ARCHITECTURAL *and* PERSPECTIVE DESIGNS

dedicated to His Majesty Charles VI, Holy Roman Emperor

by

Giuseppe Galli Bibiena

his principal theatrical engineer and architect, designer of these scenes

With an Introduction by A. Hyatt Mayor

Curator of Prints

Metropolitan Museum of Art, New York

Dover Publications, Inc., New York

Published in the United Kingdom by Constable and Company, Limited, 10 Orange Street, London W.C.2.

This Dover work, first published in 1964, contains the original title page and all the illustrations from the work titled *Architetture e prospettive dedicate alla Maestà di Carlo Sesto, Imperador de' Romani, da Giuseppe Galli Bibiena, suo primo ingegner teatrale, ed architetto, inventore delle medesime*, and published under the direction of Andreas Pfeffel in 1740. The illustrations include an allegorical drawing, a portrait of Charles VI, and fifty engravings of architectural and perspective scenes designed and drawn by Giuseppe Galli Bibiena. A new Introduction has been written especially for this edition by A. Hyatt Mayor.

Library of Congress Catalog Card Number 64-16330

Manufactured in the United States of America

Dover Publications, Inc.
180 Varick Street
New York 14, N.Y.

Introduction to Dover Edition

SOME FAMILIES stamp all their members with a resemblance so striking that the world at large gives up trying to distinguish individuals and recognizes only a composite entity. The Hapsburgs with their overripe underlip are not more alike than the Bibiena family, who, under eight names, created theatrical designs from the 1680's until the 1780's in a style so constant that their whole work looks at first glance as though it might have been done by one man at one time.

The designer of the remarkable engravings in this book was Giuseppe Bibiena (1696–1756), the happy inheritor and brilliant exploiter of the family's skills and inventions. He was born into his art and never left it for a day of his life. His father, Ferdinando (1657–1743) was the first of the eight theatrical Bibienas. He had started to design stage sets in northern Italy, and then founded the family's fortunes when he began to design stage scenery for the Hapsburgs in Vienna. The most famous teacher of this calculated and intricate kind of drawing, he summed up his experience in a book called *Civil Architecture*, which became the standard manual for generations.

When Ferdinando went to Barcelona on the family's first foreign commission, he took his twelve-year-old son Giuseppe with him. Giuseppe was sixteen when the family moved to Vienna for a stay of seven years in a court which was at that moment as extravagant and ornate as Versailles. Father and son collaborated so well that when, during a later stay in Vienna, the father went blind, the son inherited his court post as chief decorator.

Giuseppe Bibiena passed almost all of his working life in Austrian and German courts during a time when every German-speaking princeling had one passion in life—to be as grand as the French kings. Glamor was a court monopoly. A sumptuous spectacle marked each turning point of a sovereign's life, from his christening to his lying in state. If great ones did not die off fast enough at home, the deaths of royal cousins anywhere else served as occasions for piling up great catafalques of black and silver, where candles wavered as the organ shuddered in its deepest tones. God's investiture of royalty set the ruler apart from other men and cast him in a dramatic role for life.

The Church, as the oldest and wisest manager of stage effects, kept up with the times by arranging a *Theatrum Sacrum* for each festival. Those in this book are tall and narrow to fit into the court chapel in Vienna. The architecture and the figures were drawn on big flats with cutout centers. These were then set one behind the other like curtains on a Victorian window. Each flat cutout had candles to shed an indirect light on the one behind, with the brightest light falling on the farthest cutouts and the backdrop that closed the vista. Since these *Theatra Sacra* were often viewed in narrow naves and from one level, their perspective could be more rigorous and elaborate than that of theatre sets which, in spite of being calculated to look their best from the prince's central box, also had to look at least passable from right and left, from orchestra and peanut gallery.

In designing opera scenery, the Bibienas traded for a century on an innovation of Ferdinando's which opened even the tiniest stage to hitherto undreamed-of space and loftiness by painting buildings as seen at about a forty-five degree angle. A ground plan of these buildings painted on the backdrops would resemble the V of the angle of a building driving at the audience like the prow of a ship, or the upside down V of the corner of a room extending its walls to embrace the audience, or both plans combined in an X of intersecting arcades that spread outward toward the proscenium and also led back through fleeing colonnades. These restless flights of architecture running diagonally offstage toward undetermined distances revolutionized and dominated scenic design for most of the eighteenth century.

The Baroque was the supreme age of illusion. Even the Baroque mathematicians abandoned the old Greek definition of parallel lines as straight lines in the same plane that never meet, for an optical definition of straight lines that meet at infinity, as railroad tracks appear to do. Painting, by creating new illusions of roundness and new subtleties of expression, became the master art that impelled the sculptor to carve draperies that no blind man's hand could interpret, and the architect to design everything to be viewed from one level only, at which his real dimensions seem to dilate into perspective enlargements. The wise heads of the time must have seen that the new visions of space and grandeur of the stage designer, however practicable they might appear, yet remained uninhabitable dream palaces that could not but become vulgar in the solidity of stone. As the most optical of architects, the Bibienas fell heir to all the Baroque, all that Bernini and Borromini had dreamed of, but had had to leave undone. At their drawing boards, unhampered by the need for permanence, the cost of marble, the delays of masons, the whims or deaths of patrons, the Bibienas, in designs as arbitrary as the mandates of the autocrats they served, summed up the great emotional architecture of the Baroque.

The most fortunate of the eight was our Giuseppe, for he lived in the richest and most peaceful part of the century, and left us two great monuments of his unbelievable skill in the dreamlike court theatre in Bayreuth, and this book of engravings. The imperial patronage of Charles VI of Austria must have supplied the funds for reproducing Giuseppe's pen designs in the most expert and colorful engravings ever made of the drawings of any Bibiena. This is lucky for us, because practically all of Giuseppe's astonishing originals have now disappeared.

1964

A. Hyatt Mayor
Curator of Prints
Metropolitan Museum of Art
New York

ARCHITETTURE, E PROSPETTIVE

DEDICATE

ALLA MAESTA

DI

CARLO SESTO

IMPERADOR DE' ROMANI

DA

GIUSEPPE GALLI BIBIENA,

SUO PRIMO INGEGNER TEATRALE, ED ARCHITETTO,

INVENTORE DELLE MEDESIME

ÆUGUSTÆ

Sotto la Direzione di Andrea Pfeffel

MDCCXL.

Portrait of Charles VI

Martin de Meÿtens Pinxit. Andreas et Josephus Schmuzer Sculp. Vien: Austriæ.

P I.

Joseph Gali Bibiena Sac. Cæs. M. Architectus Theatralis Primariu s Inv. et del.

Andreas et Ioseph Schmuzer sc. Viennæ.

1.

P. I.

Joseph Gali Bibiena Sac. Cæs. M. Architectus Theatralis Primarius Inv. et del.

And. et Ios. Schmuzer Sc. Viennæ Austriæ.

Ioseph Galli Bibiena Primar.us Archit: S. C C. M. Inv. et delineavit.

I.A.Pfeffel S. C. M. Chalcogr. sculp. direx. A.V.

Joseph Gali Bibiena Sac. Cæs. M. Architectus Theatralis Primarius Inv. et del. *L. Zucchi sculp: Dresdæ*

6

Joseph Gali Bibiena Sac. Cæs. M. Architectus Theatralis Primarius Inv. et del.

Salomon Kleiner, Reverendiss: Elect. Moguntini Archit. Aul. sc.

Scene from the theatrical performance on the occasion of the nuptials of the Royal Prince of Poland, Prince Elector of Saxony

Scena della Festa Teatrale in occasione delli Sponsali del Principe Reale di Polonia ed Elettorale di Sassonia.

Joseph Galli Bibiena S. C. M. Archit: Theatr: Primarius Inv. et del.

L. Zucchi sculps. Dresdæ.

Joseph Gali Bibiena Sac. Cæs. M. Architectus Theatralis Primarius Inv. et del.

J. A. Pfeffel S. C. M. Chalcogr. sculp. direx. A. V.

Scene from the theatrical performance on the occasion of the nuptials of the Royal Prince of Poland, Prince Elector of Saxony

9.

Scena della Festa Teatrale in occasione delli Sponsali del Principe Reale di Polonia ed Elettorale di Sassonia.

Joseph Galli Bibiena Sac. C. M. Archit: Theatr. Primarius Inv. et del.

I. A. Pfeffel S. C. M. Chalcogr. sculp. direx. A. V.

P. I.

Ioseph Galli Bibiena Primar.[us] Archt: S.C.C.M. Inv. et delineavit.

I.A. Pfeffel S.C.M. Chalcogr. sculp. direx. A.V.

10.

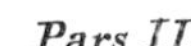

A.

P.II.

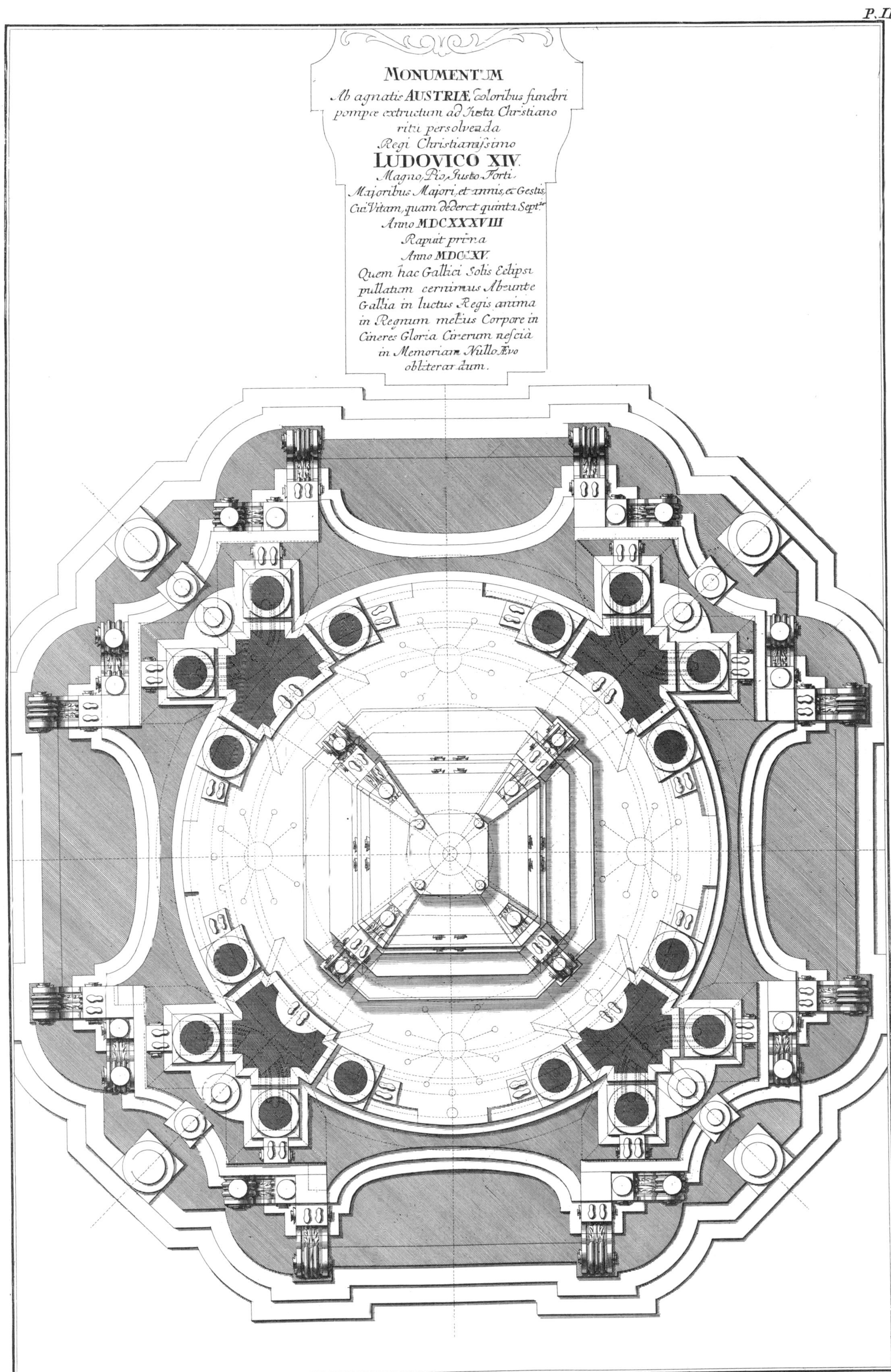

Ioseph Galli Bibienna Sac. Cæs. Maj. Architectus Theatralis Primarius Inv. et del.

I. A. Pfeffel S. C. M. Chalcogr. sculp. direx. A. V.

Et Milites plectentes Coronam imposuerunt Capiti ejus Jo. Cap. 19. v. 2

Joseph Gali Bibiena Sac. Cæs. M. Architectus Theatralis Primarius Inv. et del.

I. A. Pfeffel S. C. M. Chalcogr. sculps. direx. A. V.

Scene from the theatrical performance on the occasion of the nuptials of the Royal Prince of Poland, Prince Elector of Saxony

Scena della Festa Teatrale in occasione delli Sponsali del Principe Reale di Polonia ed Elettorale di Sassonia.

6. Joseph Galli Bibiena S.C.M. Archit: Theatr: Primarius Inv. et del.

I.A. Pfeffel S.C.M. Chalcogr. sculp. direx. A.V.

P. II.

Joseph Gali Bibiena Sac. Cæs. M. Architectus Theatralis Primarius inv. et del.

J. A. Pfeffel S. C. M. Chalcogr. sculp. direx. A. V.

Ioseph Galli Bibiena Primarius Archit: S.C.C.M. Inv. et delin. *I.A. Pfeffel S.C.M. Chalcogr. sculps. direx. A.V.*

Scene from the theatrical performance on the occasion of the nuptials of the Royal Prince of Poland, Prince Elector of Saxony

Scena della Festa Teatrale in occasione delli Sponsali del Principe Reale di Polonia ed Elettorale di Sassonia.

9 Joseph Galli Bibiena S.C.M. Archit: Theatr Primarius Inv. et del.

I.A. Pfeffel S.C.M. Chalcogr. sculp. direx. A.V.

Joseph Gali Bibiena Sac. Cæs. M. Architectus Theatralis Primarius Inv. et del.

I. A. Pfeffel S. C. M. Chalcogr. sculps. direx. A.V.

Joseph Gali Bibiena Sac. Cæs. M. Architectus Theatralis Primarius Inv. et del.

J. A. Pfeffel S. C. M. Chalcogr. sculp. direx. A.V.

P.III.

2.

Joseph. Galli Bibiena Sac. Cæs. M. Archit. Theatr. Primarius Inv. et del. — *I. A. Pfeffel S. C. M. Chalcogr. sculp. direx. A.V.*

Joseph. Galli Bibiena Sac. Cæs. M. Architectus Theatralis Primarius Inv. et del.

I. A. Pfeffel S. C. M. Chalcogr. sculpt. direx. A. V.

Joseph Galli Bibiena Sac. Cæs. Maj. Archit. Theatr. Primarius Inv. et del.

I.A. Pfeffel S. C. M. Chalcogr. sculpt. direx. A.V.

Joseph Galli Bibiena Sac. Ces. M. Archit. Theat. Primarius Inv. et del.

I. A. Pfeffel S. C. M. Chalcogr. sculpt. direx. A. V.

5.

Joseph Galli Bibiena Sac. Cæs. M. Archit. Theat. Primarius Inv. et del.

J. A. Pfeffel S. C. M. Chalcogr. sculpt. direx. A. V.

6.

P.III.

Joseph Galli Bibiena Sac. Cæs. M. Archit. Theatr. Primarius inv. et del.

I. A. Pfeffel S. C. M. Chalcogr. sculp. direx. A.V.

7.

Joseph Galli Bibiena Sac. Cæs. M. Archit. Theatr. Primarius Inv. et del. — I.A. Pfeffel S. C. M. Chalcogr. sculpt. direx. A.V.

Joseph Galli Bibiena Sac. Cæs. M. Archit. Theat. Primarius Inv. et del

J. A. Pfeffel S. C. M. Chalcogr. sculpt. direx. A. V.

P. III.

Joseph Galli Bibiena Sac. Cæs. M. Archit. Theat. Primarius Inv. et del.

I. A. Pfeffel S. C. M. Chalcogr. sculpt. direx. A. V.

10.

J. G. Bibiena Sac. Cæs. M. Architect. Theatr. Prim. Inv. et del.

J. A. Pfeffel S. C. M. Chalcogr. sculpt. direx. A. V.

1

J. G. Bibiena Sac. Cæs. M. Architect9 Theat. Prim. Inv. et del.

J. A. Pfeffel S. C. M. Chalcogr. sculpt. direx. A. V.

J. G. Bibiena Sac. Ces. M. Architect, Theat. Prim. Inv. et del.

J. A. Pfeffel S. C. M. Chalcogr. sculpt. direx. A.V.

VESTRAM, QUIRITES, PIETATEM PUBL. PRIVATAMQUE!
VIX COMPOSUISTIS S. R. IMP. IX VIRUM,
UBI EJUS FUMANTI ADHUC BUSTO
PAR OMNINO FATUM ADDIT URNAM
SERENISSIMI PRINC. AC DOMINI

DOM. IOANNIS WILHELMI

COM. PAL. RH. S. R. I. ARCHITHESAURARII ET EL. D. BAV. etc.
CÆSARI EODEM AMICITIÆ,
PROXIMIORI PATERNÆ, MATERNÆQUE COGNATIONIS VINCULO
JUNCTI.
CUI LUCTUS AUGUSTI,
OB EGREGIA IN SE ET REM PUBLICAM MERITA,
HONORIS VIRTUTISQUE CAUSÂ
MONIMENTUM,
NON OCULIS MODO VESTRIS TEMPORARIUM HOC,
SED ANIMIS ETIAM ET MEMORIÆ SEMPITERNUM
DEDICAT.

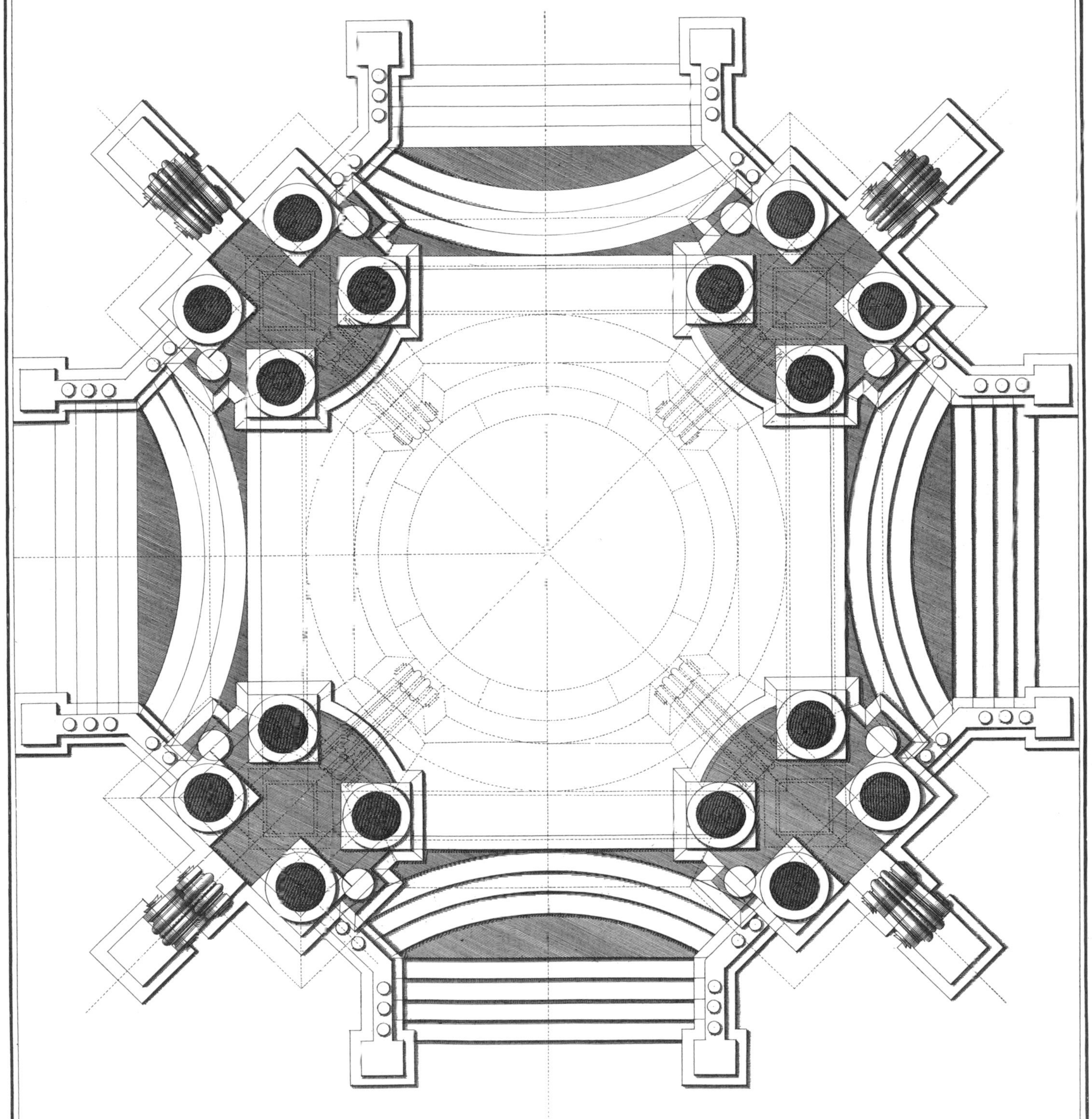

I. G. Bibiena Sac. Cæs. M. Architect. Theat. Prim. Inv. et del. *I. A. Pfeffel S. C. M. Chalcogr. sculpt. direx. A. V.*

J. G. Bibiena Sac. Cæs. M. Architect. Theat. Prim. Inv. et del.

J. A. Pfeffel S. C. M. Chalcogr. sculpt. direx. A.V.

Scene from the theatrical performance on the occasion of the nuptials of the Prince Elector of Bavaria

J. G. Bibiena S. C. M. Archit. Theatr. Prim. Inv. et del.

6.

Scena della Festa Teatrale in occasione degli Sponsali del Principe Elettorale di Baviera.

J. A. Pfeffel S. C. M. Chalcogr. sculpt. direx. A. V.

J. G. Bibiena Sac. Caes. M. Architect. Theat. Prim. Inv. et del.

J. A. Pfeffel S. C. M. Chalcogr. sculpt. direx. A.V.

7.

J. G. Bibiena Sa. Cæs. M. Architect. Theat. Prim. Inv. et del.

J. A. Pfeffel S.C.M. Chalcogr. sculpt. direx. A.V.

Scene from the theatrical performance on the occasion of the nuptials of the Prince Elector of Bavaria

9. *Scena della Festa Teatrale in occasione degli Sponsali del Principe Elettorale di Baviera.*

J. G. Bibiena Sac. Cæs. M. Architect. Theat. Prim. Inv. et del.

J. A. Pfeffel S. C. M. Chalcogr. sculpt. direx. A.V.

P.IV.

J. G. Bibiena Sac. Cæs. M. Architect. Theat. Prim. Inv. et del.

J. A. Pfeffel S. C. M. Chalcogr. sculpt. direx. A. V.

10.

Joseph Galli Bibiena Sac. Cæs. M. Archit. Theatr. Primarius Inv. et del.

J. A. Pfeffel S. C. M. Chalcogr. sculpt. direx. A. V.

Joseph. Galli Bibiena Sac. Cæs. M. Archit. Theatr. Primarius Inv. et del.

I. A. Pfeffel S. C. M. Chalcogr. sculpt. direx. A. V.

2

The covered Riding School of the Royal Court of Vienna, transformed into a salon by order of Her Majesty the Queen of Hungary and Bohemia on the occasion of the wedding of the most noble Archduchess Marianna with the most noble Prince Charles of Lorraine. This view shows one side of the hall more fully than the other; the chandeliers hanging in the center are omitted

Cavallerizza Coperta della Reale Corte di Vienna, ridotta in Sala per Comando di S. M. la Regina d'Ungheria, e di Boemia in occasione delle Nozze della Serenissima Arciduchessa Mariaña con il Serenissimo Principe Carlo di Lorena, esposta in Veduta più dà una parte, e Senza le Lumiere appese in mezzo.

3

I. G. Bibiena S. C. M. Archit: Theatr: Prim: Inv. et del.

I. A. Pfeffel S. C. M. Chalcogr. sculpt. direx. A. V.

Full-front view, as seen from the entrance, of the covered Riding School of the Royal Court of Vienna, transformed into a salon by order of Her Majesty the Queen of Hungary and Bohemia etc. etc. on the occasion of the wedding of the most noble Archduchess Marianna with the most noble Prince Charles of Lorraine. This view shows only the five chandeliers hanging in the front row; the others are omitted in order to make the drawing more clear. There were forty of these crystal chandeliers hanging in the middle of the hall, and the illumination comprised 8000 separate lights, all candles of fine wax

Facciata in veduta dall' ingresso della Cavallerizza coperta della Real Corte di Vienna, ridotta in Sala per Comando di S. M. la Regina d'Ungheria e di Boemia etc. etc. in occasione delle Nozze della Serma. Arciduchessa Marianna, con il Sermo. Principe Carlo di Lorena, esposta con le Sole 5. Lumiere appese davanti, tralasciatesi le altre per non dar confusione al Disegno. Le dette Lumiere di Cristallo appese in mezzo erano al numero di 40, e l' Illuminazione era composta di 8000. Lumi, tutte candele di Cera fina.

4

I. G. Bibiena S. C. M. Archit: Theatr. Prim. Inv. et del.

I. A. Pfeffel S. C. M. Chalogr. sculpt. direx. A.V.

Detail of one side of the same Riding School; all the festoons were made of real flowers and the backgrounds of the ornaments were gilded

Vn pezzo della Parte Laterale della medessimma Cavallerizza; tutti li festoni errano composti di fiori al Naturale, ed i fondi delli adornamenti messi ad'oro.

5

J. G. Bibiena S.C.M. Archit: Theatr: Prim. Inv. et del.

L. Zucchi sculps. Dresdæ.

J.G. Bibiena S.C.M. Archit: Theatr: Prim: Inv. et del.

J.A. Pfeffel S.C.M. Chalcogr. sculpt. et exc. A.V.

P.V.

J. G. Bibiena S. C. M. Archit. Theatr. Primarius Inv. et del.

J. A. Pfeffel S. C. M. Chalcogr. sculpt. direx. A.V.

Joseph Galli Bibiena Sac. Cæs. M. Archit. Theatr. Primarius Inv. et del.

J. A. Pfeffel S. C. M. Chalcogr. sculpt. direx. A. V.

Joseph Galli Bibiena Sac. Cæs. M. Archit. Theatr. Primarius Inv. et delin.

J. A. Pfeffel S. C. M. Chalcogr. sculpt. direx. A.V.

P.V.

J.G. Bibiena S.C.M. Archit: Theatr: Prim: Inv: et del.

J.A. Pfeffel S.C.M. Chalcogr: sculpt: direx. A.V.